Reaches

Reaches

Carroll Blair

Aveon Publishing Company

Copyright © 2001, 2011, new edition 2025 by Carroll Blair

All rights reserved. No part of this book may be reproduced, or transmitted in any form or by any means, electronic or mechanical, including photocopy, recording, or by any information storage or retrieval system without prior permission of the publisher.

ISBN: 978-1-936430-45-1

Library of Congress Control Number 2011907215

Aveon Publishing Co.
P.O. Box 380739
Cambridge, MA 02238-0739 USA

Also by Carroll Blair

Grains of Thought
Facing the Circle
Reel to Real
Shifting Tides
Out of Silence
Quarter Notes
By Rays of Light
Into the Inner Life
Gnosis of the Heart
Soul Reflections
Beneath and Beyond the Surface
Of Courage and Commitment
For Today and Tomorrow
In Meditation
Sightings Along the Journey
Through Desert's Fire
Offerings to Pilgrims
Human Natures
(Of Animal and Spiritual)
Atoms from the Suns of Solitude
Colors of Devotion
Voicings
Through the Shadows
As the World Winds Flow

It is never a chorus that gives a new melody to the world . . . coming always from the solo voice

All that Is holds the balance between yesterday and tomorrow.

It is the body that keeps one grounded to the earth. Only the body.

Everything we see will one day be no more . . . only the unseen escapes the death of our eyes.

Many times I have closed my eyes to probe the mind in search of things that would open my eyes.

The world is for man to behold, not to hold on to.

You jump up, come down, turn round and round and all remains the same; you take a step and everything changes.

Your life is forever telling you where it is going. Are you listening . . .

Sometimes speeding things up is slowing things down.

To understand one must be in the blessing of understanding.

Every moment is a once-in-an-eternity event.

All the world is in place as man goes searching for his place.

You do one thing while dreaming of another, which makes both occurrences a dream.

In time we come to know what it is we already know.

Existence exists everywhere, but *life* begins at the threshold of the profound.

Nothing dies until it begins to breathe.

One who sees only with his eyes does not see.

If the unknown did not exist man still could not know that it did not exist.

What is not acknowledged cannot be overcome.

We give ourselves away when giving nothing away.

The things in life that you are naturally drawn to . . . those are the things that belong to you, *but not the things that you own.*

It requires bread to feed the body; spiritual blood to feed the soul.

Much that follows has gone before.

One's doubts have certainties and one's certainties, doubts that one is unaware of.

The world of thunder ends in whispers.

Your name is but a reminder of who you think you are.

"If only"... yes — if only you knew how much of what happened that you wish hadn't happened, or what didn't happen that you wish had, was necessary.

You ask to be free, but do you know what you are asking for?

Some meet their tomorrows with their yesterdays; others, with more tomorrows.

What is new is never new at its beginning.

Passion moves the waves of human life, but it does not control them.

You give everyone the same things but no one receives the same things.

When you show them what you've been hiding they run and hide from you, showing you what they've been hiding.

It is in one's nothingness that one has room for all.

The wound teaches much; far more than its cure or remedy.

The highs of some spirits do not reach the heights of rapture of the lows of others.

A sufferless being would be a spiritually impotent being.

You wish the world to know who you are, but do you know who you are . . .

If you have not been where another has been in all dimensions of his or her being, how can you know where they are or where they are going . . .

And if you found what you were looking for would it still be, after that moment, what you were looking for?

You go where you want to go, do what you want to do, or so you believe.

The way is long for those who can see their way clearly.

For everything to be right some things have to be wrong.

All that comes to you joins with all that has already come.

Some hunger for a time of hunger.

There is something in life for everyone, but not for all.

He who walks alone would have many followers, if he would let them follow.

If you go to a place you've never been before and come away without having thoughts and feelings you've never had before, have you gone anywhere . . . have you been to, the place . . .

Of the true sacrifice one always gives more than the eyes of another can see.

You have reached the edge of your world and don't know what to do . . . will you turn back, or go into the abyss where no one has gone before you?

Your emptiness is filled with promise.

Is the shadow of your life friend or foe? Or both . . .

A word is spoken reaching a thousand pairs of ears, no pair hearing the same word as another.

I work toward the goal of the end of a goal and arrive at every point on the wings of a departure.

Joy goes nowhere without its pain.

Where all have gone everything's changed never to be the same.

If all were visible nothing would be seen.

It is folly to be among those who don't understand you, and who (truly) understands you . . .

You do everything and finish accomplishing nothing, not knowing that you have finished, not knowing that there is nothing.

Some people never go to their life until it is almost gone.

Always the if, the if, the If of one's life . . . of one's worth . . .

There is more than one "other world," there are many . . . some more real than the one you exist in dreaming of other worlds.

Even in the ocean one must wade through shallow waters before reaching the deep.

A ton of pain . . . an ounce of spiritual treasure.

Many speak about the world coming to an end, but has it yet come to a beginning . . .

Some follow others who move in a circle, also following them.

You appear out of nowhere . . . why so sure that you are going somewhere?

So much one needs to know before knowing he does not know.

And if you knew all that would happen tomorrow, would it still happen tomorrow . . .

To go beyond one thing that man has yet to go beyond . . . is this beyond you?

Your life needs you, but does Life . . .

Always fearful has Something been of Nothing.

The lost is found in times of loss.

Pleasure is only the wrapper of Life's true gifts.

The more the world closes in the broader becomes the *profound possibility.*

And if love would stand in your corner would you stay in your corner?

You could go to the center of a universe and it would mean nothing without reaching on the way the center of yourself.

Broken you go to others to repair you, but most want only to play with your parts.

You see nothing that hasn't been seen by another, *but the way in which you see it* has been seen by the eyes of no other.

Dreams say what they mean without concern for rhyme or meaning.

To be moved is to be pained.

What you go to soon lies behind you.

All comes from the same Place, yet from different places.

Your life has an agenda that you may or may not be aware of, may or may not assist or cooperate with, but one that you will never be allowed to interfere with.

To find your essence you must become small . . . (*very* small . . .)

We are all on our way to phenomena that as yet do not exist.

Only the past is complete.

Miracles do exist, but only amongst miracles.

Without abstraction man would understand nothing.

Everything stands accused of something.

The ice while being melted by the sun remains cold until it is no longer ice.

The spirit too needs its gravity.

Alone and more alone . . . that is how the pathway to the eternal must be journeyed.

Not everyone with their eyes closed is sleeping; not everyone with their eyes open is awake.

Some people spend their lives asking others who they are with everything they do.

You want to be something but refuse to face your nothingness — you must therefore remain as nothing

A door lies open to you but what lies behind it does not. How many doors of life have tricked you in this way . . .

Suffering is nourishment to the soul and you flee from it, starving your soul.

It is when you are feeling the most lost that you are closest to finding your way.

If some good didn't come from evil, evil could not exist.

Man was born in blood and tears like the birth of an infant . . . like a victim of war . . .

Life too, must eat . . . Life too demands its feast.

Every day worlds come apart at the seams and mend themselves before your eyes, which you do not see.

In the end it is your doubt that will save you, not certainty.

Wisdom also needs to be free.

When you have given all and can wait no longer, then will nothing be waiting for you.

Will you ever get so far as the near to you . . .

Many set sail on the ocean of Life never setting foot on the soil of their lives.

Everyone is a newborn in the presence of the unknown.

For everything that exists there is nonexistence that plays a part in the manifest of its existence.

To live without, you must live with the means of living without.

The world is more and less than what you see . . . (do you see this . . .)

The sequence of moment-to-moment existence dictates that everyone and everything is precisely where they're supposed to be at any given moment, yet so much seems out of focus . . . so much out of place . . .

Every day man shows you what he is, and you look away, as he looks away from the mirror.

You plan your life to its end without knowing what to do with this moment.

If you are not all the company you need, what company can you be (beyond the superficial) to others (beyond the superficial)?

Your love is what they need . . . not you.

"Where am I in relation to where you are?" . . . the question whispering in the distance between one and one.

If we never lost our way could it ever be found?

You journey into the world with nothing if not first having journeyed into yourself.

In the spiritual realm one plus a thousand is not the same as a thousand plus one.

How many pass by the engaging of the eternal on the way to their eternal passing . . .

Only the suffering that is great has the power to teach the greatness of its gift.

Your tragedy may be a prelude to the sublime.

You make way for what comes your way not realizing that it wants you to meet it, sometimes embrace it, sometimes challenge it.

What has been granted to you could never have been if not for what has been denied you.

To not realize that all that you've experienced has been necessary to your life is to not realize the necessities of your life.

To be more you must do more. Are you ready to do more?

Many fear the call of death summoning them, but even more fear the call to Life.

What treasures of mind and heart could many a spirit find if not so afraid of finding them.

A day of rest is known least to one who is his own master.

You go inside yourself and find nothing and are disappointed, not realizing that you must build the inner life before it can be found.

What awaits at the highest peak of spiritual enlightenment is not comforting peace but suffering filled with beauty and joy beyond imagining.

And is that what you thought freedom was, to be free from the pains of living; of thought, of feeling, of life? . . .

In the sense that you are part of everything it is not wrong to see yourself in everything, but you are not satisfied — you want to *be* everything, which brings you to the rule of nothing.

What you want to be is not who you are; – what others need you to be is not who you are; – who are you . . .

The best of what you are cannot surface, because you always want to show others your best.

Some defend themselves against rejection, others, against acceptance.

Your future arrives with your signature.

What was long ago will become clearer tomorrow.

Of all that man applauds the world remains silent.

Man, still in his infancy, fleeing from God, still in His infancy.

Dividing time . . . like dividing the flow of the river.

It is only space that separates, and space is nothing.

All that is seen is the result of an explosion of something that no one can see.

The visible is but a shadow of the Invisible.

In the beginning everything was the same.

All motion leads to possibility and away from possibility.

A moment is no less than forever; forever, no greater than a moment.

The reach to stillness is beyond the speed of light.

Hell's fire is most intense before the gates of Paradise.

Not everything falls into place . . . some things rise . . .

Some are spared sufferings so they may know Suffering.

The highest pain and the highest joy meet on the same summit and embrace.

In the spiritual it is sometimes wound healing wound.

Spiritually speaking the fullest cup is the cup that runneth over with emptiness.

How many gifts silence brings to the mind receptive to its calling (!) . . .

The straightest path is the narrowest path.

It requires genius to see what is *right in front of you.*

What we do would not be possible if not for all that we do not do.

Of some things, to serve is to master.

A failure of understanding shared by many is that to live more one must die more.

Whatever can be taken from you was never yours to keep.

You complain of what is denied you while that which lies open to you stays ignored like fruit waning in the sun.

When your back is to a corner the whole world lies before you, and you think of only the corner.

How often when others came to you, you felt that they were leaving you and you, them, when going to them . . .

You have seen humankind for what it is. Will you now have the courage to go on living as human . . .

Perhaps life has whispered to man "time's up" many times, but man was not listening.

The spirit also has its seasons. In which do you now exist?

And if everything ended at this moment would you still appreciate the treasure of the moment?

You search and search and cannot find what you are looking for, because you are too much in the way of what you are looking for.

Life only takes back what it gives, transformed.

Sometimes reality follows you into your dream and you think you are only dreaming.

All things save a secret for themselves.

To be filled with nothing but question is to be infinitely richer than to be filled with answer and certainty.

The shallow are closer to the light than those who dwell in the depths, *but they never look up to see it.*

Some prefer a strong uncertainty to a weak security, which preserves the security of their soul.

The world of abstraction too is a world of round.

Everywhere life goes it leaves beginnings of ends and ends of beginnings . . .

The mind owns everything that the eyes have seen.

In a world void of meaning one may still discover a world of meaning.

Suffering is not your enemy.

The profound silence says everything that ever needs to be said.

Some are given riches beyond measure, but are poor because they do not recognize them.

The way to the ranks that bear wings is as it were forging on foot with heavy load through desert fog.

So many disrupt the Possibility of their possibilities.

They most want to belong who least belong to themselves.

Some people go from heart to heart hoping to gain entrance like an orphan going from door to door.

No one expects you to be yourself, only the self that he or she wants you to be.

People placing people, like children placing their toys in a box . . . because people love their toys, and they need their box.

You let yourself go and wonder why you are not moving, forgetting those who hold onto you, never letting you go.

They go to you believing they are free, believing you are free, the invisible chains silent in their strengthening.

You do not know them because they stay, and they stay because they fear if they leave, you will never know them.

And if you saw the lost of the beloved again, would you *see* them, or would you be seeing yourself looking at them looking at you . . .

It is in the pauses of your speech where I understand what you are saying.

You have all you wanted but now you want something more — all you forgot that you need.

While you are deciding things about your life your life is deciding things for you.

You look forward and face from where you have come.

The world opens up to you and asks nothing in return. What will you give it in return . . .

The search for happiness is not the search that has the most to teach you.

And is that what you've been looking for, a state of being where you need not look any further?

He will never reach himself who never journeys away from himself.

The real thing has, because of its rarity, an air of the unreal.

For most the familiar is as unknown as the unfamiliar, the visible as unknown as the invisible.

Of some things one must also earn the right to earn the right to them.

Shallow is shallow, but depth has many depths.

It is the wisest minds that have the most to teach, but also the most to learn.

If what man refers to as suffering did not exist man would suffer even more.

What would be best for all can never be for all.

The highest things hold no weight upon them, but upon themselves the highest spirits carry the heaviest burdens.

One's task is not great whose suffering is not great.

They seem smallest to themselves who cast the longest shadows.

They think they are something, who have never experienced their nothingness, who must do so before they can be . . . something.

The noble go to life and world with open heart forever emptying it to keep it full, returning with nothing . . . (i.e., with everything).

To the creator, death is only a thought.

One gets a closer look at things when one is alone . . . when there is no one around to block one's vision.

One grows most silent when one has most to say.

Words open and close the doors of understanding always moving . . . always.

As you think of the future it has already come and gone.

What you have done shows you where you have been.

Sometimes the great gift is something taken from one rather than something given.

Each life too is a puzzle which requires that one strive if all the pieces are to be put in the right place.

Holding on to one's realities is more difficult than holding on to one's dreams.

Things may change permanently, but there is no such thing as a permanent change.

The visible is ruled by the invisible.

It is not Death but Life that takes away life.

To be part of existence is something that one may cherish or not cherish, may honor or not honor, but it is something that no one has ever asked for.

Nature says the same things in its way over and over again — (but not *quite* the same things . . .)

The sun conceals as much as it reveals.

The spiritual light of some is so bright that others cannot see it and condemn them, believing they exist without light.

Wisdom closes doors as well as opens them.

The spiritually brave let not the world get in the way of their world.

Some people live their whole life as an apology.

Reality is ever close at hand, but how many rush off to the call of Illusion . . .

A life falls between the cracks creating the cracks through which it has fallen . . .

Man becomes most aware of his nothingness when he tries to fill it with the illusionary.

No one reaches the end of one's truth, but many never reach its beginning.

As long as man believes he is going somewhere he will continue to go nowhere.

How can a life be lost if it was never one's to keep . . .

How quickly do the blind lead those to see who are capable of seeing.

All that is must be because of all that has been.

What lives beyond the day is paid for with the day.

Nothing exists without its shadow.

Not all shadows are perceptible.

Pleasure doesn't always smile, nor does pain always frown.

Beautiful things do not come from only the beautiful.

You are part of something that is miraculous, but are you miraculous . . .

Do you love the many things that make up the whole, or the whole that consists of the many things?

What have you learned from what you have learned . . .

Is what you understand in the blood of your understanding?

Truth . . . how much of it do you dare to face . . . how much of it do you dare to tell . . .

To know all would be to suffer all.

You come to the world as you are, but do you go everywhere (or anywhere) as you are . . .

Many believe that the world has abandoned them when it is they who have abandoned themselves.

The journey to oneself is always a journey of one taken by one.

If you want to be more you need to want less.

It is okay to leave behind those who have fallen behind you . . . this you must do if you are to help them . . . if they are to help you.

Will you know what to do when life comes to claim you?

You want to cleanse your soul but are afraid to give anything up, to let anything go.

Your life's suffering has paid for the moment you are now living and with it you fail to live.

You're too independent, you say, for the game of follow the leader. You choose instead to follow the follower.

They believe they know where you are going without knowing themselves where they're going or from where they are coming.

You carry around many things not realizing how many of them are carrying you.

Nothing in Nature ever looks back — only man looks back.

Spiritually speaking there are suns in the depths more scorching than the star that lights the surface of the earth.

In the inner world too is something sometimes saved by the destruction of something else.

Only the shattered can truly be known.

And if the price of life were nothing, would it be worth more than nothing?

All have a crossing of no return.

Man has spoken billions of words and still cannot find the words.

Profound pain leads to profound truth.

Is it worth the understanding, what is easy to understand?

And if the world were as you say, what then would you dare say . . . not say . . .

Is not the temporal the dream and the eternal the reality . . .

Man is born whole and goes to his death as almost nothing.

Mysteries are not veiled in obscurity but glow in clarity too sharp to be seen.

They are as ghosts on the earth who live without illusions.

Some say no and give us Yes.

More powerful than a thousand tears is a single tear.

To have no need to need, no want to want . . . is this not what the highest souls need, what the highest souls want?

Every day is different, but never changing its way.

The world is nameless despite the names it's been given, and man continues to give names in his name.

The death of a century is no match for the life of a moment.

Reason can be a great deceiver . . . (perhaps the greatest deceiver of all).

You say that you are at peace with yourself, but are you at peace with your peace?

The more distant the spiritual journey the lighter one must travel.

The light can be more blinding than the dark.

And if the night of your life suddenly came upon you would you offer it your sun?

Do you believe that love conquers all, and is that what you want, to be conquered?

You are an entity of never-was and never-to-be-again between all there was and will ever be.

A river without its banks is not a river.

What one hasn't the eyes to see one cannot see.

Life brings nothing to man. It is man who must bring everything to life.

Are you an arrow seeking a bow or a bow seeking an arrow?

Nothing can be held onto that is not let go.

What I conceive today I could not possibly have conceived yesterday nor could I conceive tomorrow.

I discovered my beliefs by travelling the road of nonbelief.

Some of what my eyes have looked upon I see only now.

The idea that I will one day be no more is easier to comprehend than the fact that I am.

We seem important to ourselves until we look up — then everything seems important except ourselves.

You put aside living and tend to the business of life. You have learned the value of life.

A perfect bliss is not a perfect happiness or perfect joy.

The sun does not shine for itself.

Is not the sky more beautiful with clouds than without them, and also life?

Everyone has afflictions that they cannot do without.

A world without suffering would be the most insufferable world of all.

The world is fooled by nothing; man by almost everything.

The Grand Mystery is the mystery of Reality.

A pebble drops in the ocean . . . the ocean never the same.

How moved one may become by the stillness of silence.

A thousand times I have gone to the edge of my mind and a thousand times it has urged me to go further.

Sometimes when I leave the irrational out of my reasoning
I feel that something important is missing.

The way is far longer to reach the nothing of ourselves than it is
to reach the something of ourselves.

Knowledge is a hindrance for one who yearns to know all
things.

How much of life is missed by participating in it.

For all to be as it is every entity must be as it is.

Nothing is part of everything.

The face of naked Existence . . . what could be more terrifyingly beautiful to set one's eyes upon . . .

Freedom . . . a concept that everyone talks about and no one understands.

Light cloaks its essence on a cover of darkness.

The future, ever coming; the present, ever passing; the past, forever gone . . . what is to be made of it all . . .

The fractions of time sense no difference between themselves.

A world of difference never makes all that different a world.

If you did all there was to do there would be nothing left for you to do — but you would still go on doing.

Some people need a lifetime to show you who they are, others but a moment.

Who can be sure that one is living the life of one's choosing . . .

One's dreams too are a part of one's reality.

It is beyond your power to destroy what cannot be taken from you.

And do you have the courage to do it, to embrace what won't go away . . .

Life moves on with or without you.

There is no shortcut to the sublime.

Nothing weighs more heavily on one's being than the weight of one's nothingness.

All spiritual fortune is created by one — (i.e., by an individual).

What can he not face who can face himself . . .

Light will always find its way into the places of soul that one allows it to go.

Never will Truth be found in a crowd.

No one can pay a spiritual debt for another.

Of anything, no two benefit the same from the same amount.

The world never explains.

How much the daydreamer often sees when staring into the distance looking at nothing.

Before Wisdom Knowledge bows its head and remains silent.

Where there is spiritual suffering there is love.

What should be taken seriously that hasn't risen from a bed of thorns . . .

Their hands are full, their bellies are full, their pockets are full . . . everything but their minds and hearts.

When they cannot hear what you are saying why do you go on saying . . .

Heaven is not for the faint of heart.

Only the spiritually evolved can recognize the spiritual treasure of another.

It is pain, not pleasure that moves one to take the first step toward discovery beyond the superficial.

When things are made harder for the great artist or saint it makes it easier for them to follow their path.

The world's shadow follows those who do not follow the world.

What is the reason for being if not to create a reason for being?

And if all would stop believing in themselves would you stop believing in yourself?

Many eyes have looked upon you, but how many have seen you . . .

You build walls around you, but the walls have doors, and the doors are unlocked.

What can you give them who go to you with everything inside of nothing . . .

In matters of the heart no one can retrieve for another what he or she has lost.

There are those who cannot bear silence but want to know the profound — they will never know it.

Man needs not half of what he wants.

There are worlds of love, but not a world of love.

Evil too is forever young.

It is the devil who laughs when hearing the voices of angels.

When man is not more than an animal, he is less than an animal.

It is a long road to becoming, something . . .

Life holds no one to the promise of one's life.

Tragedy burns wisdom into the sensitive soul.

One man acquires many things and has gained nothing; another lets go of many things and gains everything.

Man *deserves* almost nothing.

And if it all came apart would you deny (like Peter) that you were ever a part . . .

You are in error to assume that life needs to be good to you to grant you a good life experience.

In the heart of one's being one learns what love is saying.

The voice within is more *felt* than heard . . .

One travels far to find the very near.

The most far-reaching spirits are the most solitary.

The way out of yourself is the way into yourself.

Spiritually speaking there are eyes that can see in the darkest of tunnels and will not blink in the face of the sun.

The dawn is born of the night without break between darkness and light.

It requires the utmost calm to attract thought that brings lightning and thunder.

To honor is futile when not honoring the eternal.

All but the timeless is hollow.

One must see or experience the unbelievable before one can (truly) *believe*.

You turn away from your life to face Life . . . when you turn back will your life still be there, i.e., the life that you have known . . .

You slow your pace and simplify in hope that they will better understand, and they understand less.

And if you knew that there was nothing waiting for you at the end of your journey would you have the courage to go on, reaching for the finish?

You wonder where all the fruit has come from, forgetting the seeds of your suffering, then finally, your suffering.

Only pain can speak with authority.

The last thing to be taken from a life is its shadow.

Realities must often be imagined before they can be discovered.

To know that there is something more, even without knowing what it is, is to know more.

The ignorance of some knows better than the knowledge of others.

It is not only before strangers where one must sometimes remind oneself that one is standing before strangers.

An individual is more of a riddle than life itself.

You cannot go with them, nor they with you into those places where they find themselves, and you find you.

You enter a place and do not see what you are looking for, failing to see the world that is in its place.

And do you know what you have done on the way to yourself, overlooking the things that are worth more than yourself . . .

You want someone to help you – he turns away from you – you sigh with disappointment not realizing that he has helped you.

One cannot grow to great heights who has not fallen to great depths.

The qualities about you that you have the most reason to be proud of could not be without your afflictions.

Suffering deepens, but courage is needed to explore the depths that it creates.

In the spiritual realm one is pursued by that which one pursues.

To be all that you are takes everything that you are.

As you approach the future it looks over your shoulder into your past to see how you should be greeted and what experiences must now be prepared for you.

"What does life want from me?" "Everything you have."
"But what do I owe to life?" "More than you have."

The more alone one is the more the world lies open for one to see.

Great things put little things to shame, always to shame . . . life grants no choice in the matter.

Man's good is like the day; sometimes bright, sometimes gray, sometimes dark; – his evil like the night — always dark.

They themselves commit an evil who help others to avoid confronting their evil.

What do they know of the light who have never battled the demons of the dark . . .

Many go in search of anything but themselves.

Some pave their paradise with stone and wonder why it is turning to stone.

There are people who can expand their consciousness, but not *raise* it.

No human life is without need of correction.

They are furthest from reality who are most sure of what reality is.

The daydream is called many things.

How clearly everything appears to the confused, and confused to those who see clearly.

The outer life is but a shadow life pursued with vigor by the shallow.

Some people spend their lives following dreams they never dream.

Spiritually speaking one evolves slowly toward the lightning that strikes in a flash.

How much spiritual blood (unseen) has gone up in smoke (unseen) consumed by spiritual fire (invisible . . .)

The heart is master to that which is able to wound it, slave to that which it is able to wound.

The mind too has its eyes its ears its hands its nose its tongue.

Not to man will it ever be known of all that man is.

No two carry within them the same world.

Eyes must bleed before they can take in all that they see.

There are times when the enlightened have no place to go but into the darkness.

All that is seen is a veil to the unseen.

To give up nothing would be to sacrifice nothing, but to give up your nothingness would be to sacrifice everything.

What beautiful and profound creations may manifest from the sacred space of Emptiness . . .

The soul too is something that must be cultivated, that must be grown.

You lose something to the world found by no one; but is it lost to the world . . .

Sometimes it's as if you wake as the world goes to sleep and go to sleep as the world awakens.

Is your dream a place of rest, or a place where demons crack their whips . . .

You are strong in your desire to be strong, but are you strong enough to allow your weakness to take part in the building of your strength . . .

After life . . . after death . . . what is the difference?

Anyone who doesn't impede your journey helps you along on your journey (though they never move an inch to help you).

And is that the measure of your love, to love only the loveable . . . then you do not know love.

The world always has more than what you hope for, but sometimes less of what it is you are hoping for.

Everyone takes some spiritual debt to their grave.

Some must sing for their supper; others must die for their song.

Suffering is more friendly when it is greeted with open arms.

Every birth demands its pain and blood.

Only the spiritually evolved know what it means to graduate from oneself.

What is the sense of wanting to go anywhere spiritually speaking if not always wanting to go further?

You go on without them, they go on without you, taking more of them with you and they more of you than if you continued the journey together.

No two spirits freeze or burn at the same temperature.

Every life has a beginning and an end, but what of Life . . .

A million search, but only one truly knows what he is searching for.

In spirituality a little darkness is also needed to shade the light.

It is in caves of ice where the hottest springs are to be found.

An army of rules comes to a journey's start — they're met with one, and lay down their arms.

That which man is not is the space to his spiritual world that allows for movement and expression of all that he is or will ever be.

Some spirits are rich in their poverty, others poor in their wealth.

The more who gather to celebrate something the more the feeling that something's been lost.

What escapes the awareness of one is captured by another.

Sometimes for something to be going your way it must be moving in a direction away from you.

If everything were the same life would have no place to go.

The good that man believes exists in the world does exist, but not in the measure that he believes it exists.

The vaguest movements are the longest lived.

To be grateful for what you have gained is to owe gratitude to all you have been denied.

You have grown but feel out of place because those around you have not grown. Why do you not see *them* as out of place . . .

The world has no desire to see anything, yet how many spend their lives showing the world what they think it wants to see.

To understand one must not participate; to participate one must not understand.

Oh the Great Error of collective "reality" . . . .

Who attracts the herd speaks the language of the herd.

Will you be among the brave of humankind, turning away from the safety of its lie to the danger of its truth . . .

You asked no one permission to be born. Why ask anyone how you shall live?

The eagle trusts her wings.

Many doors one must close or be closed to one before the gates of paradise open before him.

And if the story of a life is not the story of its work, is it a story that lives beyond the shallows . . .

One is part of all that one seeks.

In the world of spirituality money is a beggar.

Some want to show others what they have to prevent them from looking at what they are.

One cannot *ask* to be loved or believed in.

They notice least of the world who most want the world to notice them.

If one has never been in awe of life what could one possess that would inspire the sense of awe in others?

One is the measure of one's heart, the substance of one's mind, the essence of one's soul.

What have they learned of lasting value who have never used their temporal existence to explore the eternal?

To get to one's whole spiritually speaking requires at every step to leave a piece of oneself behind.

If you never turn away from the world how can you bring it to something new . . .

How much of you is in what you have given to life? And do you think it matters . . .

Some must wait until they have nothing left to give to give the best that they have.

One falls only so far as his courage allows him to fall.

What you feel you *must* do . . . that is what *you* must do.

One who is held prisoner by his past is held by phantom guards.

Sometimes people pretend that they are pretending.

The songs of some lives are too well rehearsed to play well.

Many want others to speak to them, but few want to listen.

Stories never told are stories that never end.

Some go to others with open arms but not open heart, and want to be received with open heart.

You take a child by the hand and go for a walk exploring the natural world, and by the end of the journey it is the child taking you by the hand . . .

A child thinks the morning arrives for her. It does . . . some adults think it arrives for them. Perhaps . . . depends . . .

What day is consistent with the next?

No one searches harder for reality than the dreamer.

Sometimes to add something to life one must for a time forget life.

Silence . . . the womb of sublime conception.

It is in the distance between you and another that the substance of your union exists.

At every moment you are where you need to be to do what you need to do.

In the spiritual realm one is a hindrance to oneself. One must put oneself out of the way if the way to truth, to love, to grace is to be found.

The ability to love includes the ability to be (if need be) without love.

You cannot see the tears of the world when your eyes are wet with tears.

What gnaws at the soul does not limit its preying to only the soul.

The best things are hidden, but out in the open; yet only the eye of the open heart is able to perceive them.

Behind shattered dreams lie visions of tomorrow.

Every experience of spiritual suffering is one step closer to the light (or greater light).

What is worth having that is not paid for with our lives day by day, hour by hour, minute by minute . . .

If your time is now it is not for always.

One acquires no thought, no lesson, no insight or vision that one hasn't earned.

They will never have anything more who give everything to what they already have.

In the spiritual dimension even more than in the physical, there is always work to be done.

The great spirit is ever consumed with a passion for what is greater than itself.

Cold are the ashes of passions expired.

Eternal light could never be if not for the presence of eternal darkness.

Because I love the silence in my life I do not fear the silence of death.

I use this corporal life which is grounded in change to find my way to the spiritual unchanging.

Obsession . . . the fuel of one's dreams.

Sometimes I must close my eyes so I can see more clearly.

I do not love suffering, but I do the blessings that it brings.

"Go to the pain," my spirit tells me . . . "that's where life *begins*."

The eye of the storm . . . how beautiful it must be.

Every moment is the dawn of an eternity.

You thought you were falling, but all the while it was a world rising before you.

Beneath the surface everything is paradoxical.

It is possible to doubt, yet still embrace.

The road to simplicity is filled with complexity.

One can accomplish only that which one can endure.

One must ultimately take life whole into one's heart, into one's soul or one goes away with nothing.

I have come to the end of a beginning.

ABOUT THE AUTHOR

Carroll Blair is an author of more than twenty books and the recipient of numerous awards. His work has been well endorsed and commendably reviewed. Among his titles cited for distinction are *Through the Shadows*, winner of the Pacific Book Awards, and *Quarter Notes*, winner of the Sharp Writ Book Awards. He is an alumnus of the Boston Conservatory and lives in Massachusetts.

www.ingramcontent.com/pod-product-compliance
Lightning Source LLC
Chambersburg PA
CBHW031403040426
42444CB00005B/405